A WALK THROUGH LIFE

YVONNE CRIST

ISBN: 979-8-9907665-4-9 (paperback)
ISBN: 979-8-9907665-5-6 (eBook)

INKTRAIL PRESS

CRAFTING STORIES, INSPIRING READERS

To my darling beloved husband who died recently on August 23rd of last year, my handsome sons, Patrick and Daniel, and my beautiful & dedicated sisters, Paula, Catherine, and Sinead, who gave me strength and love to find my way home.

Written in honor of our parents, my sweet sister Sinead, and our beloved brother, Eamonn.

Special regards to Louise, my darling friend, who gave me encouragement and hope.

Contents

Preface... ix
Introduction xi

Walking in my Power... 1
Life.. 2
Disappointment! 3
Death 4
Dad 5
Mom 6
Parents... 7
Brother of Mine 8
Broken heartedness 9
You are Gone! 10
His Kiss.. 11
Resting with Angels 12
Sis Sinead... 13
Heart's Desire.. 14
When I look at you. 15
What to Do? 16
Broken 18
The Pain 19
Splintering of Self... 20
Rage.. 21
Lost... 22
The Future 24
Kindness 25

Mental Health 26

Coming Home 27

Forgiveness 28

Yet I Am Worthy 29

Relationship 30

Life's Dream 31

I Have Found the One My Soul Doth Love.............. 32

How Do I Love Thee? 33

Intoxication! 34

My Love 35

Family 36

It Is Well with My Soul.................................. 37

Health Is Wealth 38

Abiding Love 39

Imagine 40

"Let there be light."................................... 41

God's Love 42

Letting Go and Letting God 43

Prayer 44

Spring Is Here 45

Hope 46

Faith... 47

Grace 48

Compassion 49

Trust... 50

Respect 52

Honesty 53

Wisdom.. 54

Humility 55

Happiness 56

Joy 57

Empathy 59

Gratitude.. 60

Patience 61

Strength... 62

Self-Esteem 63

Courage 64

Soul's Journey 65

Soul's Light 66

Soul's Peace 67

Feelings.. 68

War 69

Our World Today.. 70

Awaken World! 71

Sisters 72

Paula..73

Catherine 74

Friend...75

Pastor Lynn 76

Louise Catherine 77

Molly.. 78

Thought 79

Rain... 80

Twilight 81

Beauty Moon.. 82

Daylight Bright.. 83

Here Comes the Sun 84

Blessings 85

Preface

Poetry is my avenue to express my inner thoughts and feelings about what touches my heart and soul. In this book, there are poems written at pinnacle turning points in my life and I was inspired to write. I know you will discover yourself immersed in some of these poems as they bring you into a realm of deep, reflective understanding. Others delve deeper, expressing my own relationship with God. They are poems of encouragement, deep reflection, sustenance, love, and hope.

Life is a journey that takes time, so be kind to yourself and others, for you will be blessed.

Introduction

I stand looking in the mirror and see a woman who has finally made peace with herself. I now see an authentic woman and I love the entirety of me. It has been a long and arduous journey through streams, rocky hillsides, high mountain ranges, and torrent waterfalls, trekking forward, till finally coming to rest in green pastures. I have come to realize that I am a resilient and brave person. My heart is still beating, and I radiate with a deeper insight. Now I stand in the sunlight and beam. Sixty-four years now, and as I look back through the years of time, I reflect on images that were shadowed in turmoil. I smile and appreciate my qualities. It has taken me this long to wash away the stings of briars, muddied clothing, and soggy boots to accept I am well. And with lives gone, coming to terms with how precious life truly is.

Dealing with mental illness, feeling sad, lonely, miserable, bitter, and being filled with fear was treacherous and brewed a steamy, hot, veiled anger.

All I knew was heightened hypervigilance and the anxious ticking of the clock. Dreaded fear of not being good enough, frightened fear of what was coming around the corner, and terrified fear of losing my mind. Fearing fear would writhe my body back and forth till the pills abated all sensation.

Death was waiting, lurking in the shadows, and its scythe cut swift like a hawk.

I chose to leave my children and my divorced husband. I flew away from my silent family to far distant lands to a home where I believed I could rest my weary head and body. The choice I made almost buried me. Anguish grasped my disillusioned, maddening mind.

Darkness...

   Crawling out of my tomb of despair took every ounce of will, to want to live again. I peeked some days through the windows, only to fall back into oblivion. I gradually set each foot down with trepidation until eventually I could stand, slowly beginning to walk. I garnered the strength to face life head-on. My guilt, anger, bitterness, fear, shame, and silence that had been suffocating me, spiraled slowly down, like tiny, slivered pieces of rusted steel over the long years of grief. Death gives meaning to living. It is the great leveler. There is no better teacher in life than death. I am alive, breathing, smiling, and I am secure in myself. My self-respect returned. I cherish my loved ones daily and keep them close to my beating heart. Finally, I am me again. I remarried my husband and that was the happiest day of my life. I found my belonging and I was family once again.

   Now, I am deeply shattered to write that my darling husband, Richard, left this world on August 23rd recently, at his home, surrounded by his loving family; I am so saddened in my heart that this was the hardest blow in my my life and now all is empty; My life preserver is no longer with me and I am left holding the pieces together to my life without him; I cannot tell you how much this person was my world; I love you my sweetheart, and may you rest easy with God.

Weep no more and take the shroud from thy face.
See life abounding and embrace life's grace.
Everyone is calling you to leap and dance,
And feel happy to welcome all happenstance.

Walking in my Power

When you have walked in my shoes, you will understand how
    prevailing I am.
How I met each sting and each swarming bee with a commanding
    spirit, without being a sham.
When you come to know my mountains and valleys, you will find
    some grace within.
How when faced with adversity, I still crawled to remain true to a
    commitment to win.
When you listen and hear all I have to say, I feel you will realize
    my own contentment.
My life has been a struggle, but you will see how far I have come
    to enjoy my own betterment.
My will and determination have proven the strength and
    resilience I hold.
And my own courage is bolden red, full to the brim of gratitude
    and a firm foothold.
You and I have a story to tell, one that will rock all others into
    power.
For you and I have sat and listened and found a common ground
    to flower.

Life

It is unexpected.
It is a moment in time.
It is rich and living within a paradigm.

It is a gift, a climb to the staircase of heaven,
And when you tremble, walk fully into the sun.
And enjoy its rays, with gracious progression.

Life's out there, longing for your embrace.
Life's everywhere; see it lit upon your face.

Life can fall to the depths of despair.
And crumble into a million pieces.
But there is nothing you cannot bear, with a little prayer,
As time and rhythm never ceases.

Life is a blessing, not a curse!
Be a part of this world for better or worse!
Life's not fair, but see, life is everywhere.

Make a stance! Take a chance!
Share You with the world.
Roll out your red carpet, see what unfurls.
Give! Have no regrets.

Be that person, no one forgets!

Disappointment!

Never think that your life will turn out truly as imagined.
Never feel that your path will furrow as fashioned.

Never believe all that you have wanted
Will be granted to you, undaunted.

Never doubt that the people you intermingle with,
Will pose as hurdles forthwith.

Never imagine that the world is your oyster.
Always ponder life, like silky threads of gossamer.

Never abuse the people you meet.
Never naively believe, with conceit.

Always consider and deliver!
Question! Have discretion!

Never be late for a friend or an appointment.
Otherwise, disappointment!

Death

Death so poignant, heartbreaking, and final.
You come at your own time; You have no rival.
Earthshaking, heart-wrenching pain, forsaking none,
You gather souls with spirit slipped on.
You spread your wings earnestly,
As You journey fervently.

I embrace your dignity,
And ache with affinity.
Sobered by your nobleness.
I cry with humble mournfulness.

I hold you in awe.
But still feel raw.
How I wish it were not final.
Though I feel no reprisal.
For death was their wish.
Thus, surrendered them to You, by my tender kiss.

Dad

Where has the time flown, when once I sat on your knee?
Where have the years gone, when first you laid eyes on me?
Where have the days dwindled, from whence you gave me the
    first kiss?
Oh, how my heart aches, while I reminisce.

When I was young, you braved the world,
Providing safety, that surged unfurled.
But see, I am strong now and holding my own,
Still loving you solely, amid this heartbreaking milestone.

How I cherish your love,
And thank you for your guidance,
By bringing me home, to true love's alliance.
And now our lives are forever marked with your touch,
Showing us that family truly means so much.

How I feel your heart aglow,
And within your precious heart, our gardens grow.

Mom

I came not knowing what to expect.
Fear and apprehension filled my soul.
And then I saw and knew with respect
That you were ready to meet your heart's celestial goal.

You proved me right,
As the time came to say goodbye.
And your soul shone bright,
As you joined Dad in the Heavenly sky.

Loving being present and giving succor, all I could,
You showed us all how dying is for good.
You gave me life, the gift beyond all measure.
T'was a meek and humbling time together.

I love you with all my heart.
For you are my mother, my treasure.
The time for me was precious till I saw you depart.
A time that will always live with me forever.

Parents

You were the heart, the beat, the rhythm.
We are the part of God, who hath given
The light of His glory unto us, and it showed,
By your loving hearts, that our lives flowed.

You were the mentors of all that is true.
We are the result of your counsel that grew.
You were the teachers, the faith, and the meaning.
We are the trees who grew strong, while you were still breathing.

You were the reason for our living.
You were our warmth, that flowed without ceasing.
You were the thought, the joy, and why we coped.
We are your mirrors, your shining hope.

You were the ones who bore and carried all.
You were our shelter when we would fall.
We regarded how you felt and heeded what you meant.
You were the rock on which we leant.

Brother of Mine

Through your eyes, your light shone like a beacon,
That awakened your life force, which did not weaken.
Through your heart, your warmth glowed warmer than the sun,
And helped to infuse the living souls of everyone.
Through your spirit, your rays soothed all the pains of heartaches
    we sustained.

Through your fingertips, your kindness touched us,
And filled our lives to a maximum plus.
Through the years, your compassion glimmered,
And brought a harmony pleasing that shimmered.
Through the future, you will still be my friend.
The one who cared deeply, ceaselessly, without end.

You were the keeper, the guardian of all.
You were the sense, the wisdom we recall.
You were the giver, the Heart that loved so.
You were the brother who never said no!

Broken heartedness

You have left this world, Eamonn, which for us is now achingly
    surreal!
You, laid still, pulled the trigger, and with a resounding peal, It
    rang through the silence of your broken heartedness!

Oh, how our hearts ache and long for you here,
But reality crashes through our tears.
Reminding us that you can no longer be with us, for you lie in dust.
Even our entreats to hold you, are crushed.

Often, I think of how you must have felt, just before
You broke your solitude, to live no more!

Oh, the tremendous pain, upon pain, upon pain.
To accept you are truly gone, never to awaken again.

Looking up, I think of you, and wonder how you are!
Maybe peaceful, happy, or a shining twinkling star.
We will always remember you, Eamonn, our darling brother,
As God helps us through the mire of daily living without you,
    your heart a blazon, warm as fire.
Sorrow is still ours now, as there will be *no other*.

You are Gone!

You are gone!
No longer a living part of our lives!
Vanishing into the mists of our minds!
Tinkling at times, like a song!

You are no longer here. Oh, but to have you near.
Alas your death crashes through our tears,
Reminding us, we must labor through our remaining years.

Wishing only to have the chance,
To steal a glance,
Or to hug you and dance,
Perchance!

Understanding is ours; for we no longer hear your beautiful voice.
Sadly, you made the choice,
To end the pain, you lived over and over and over again.

However, God says "No! He is My son now!
So be at peace, somehow.
For I do hold him, tenderly in My arms,
Beloved; singing his melodious charms."

His Kiss

I am well now, free, and with my family.
I am filled with happiness and fear is no more.
My soul has soared heavenward, conjoining spiritually.
God comforts me, imbuing me with His Precious Love's core.

The gifts of peace, joy, and completeness abound.
I am One with my Father now, for all eternity.
My life story profound.
I am no longer wound to my physical and emotional duality.

I am loved, welcomed and reborn.
For now, my redemption is made.
And in this knowledge, my soul is no longer forlorn.
The joy of this communion comes from His kiss immediately laid.

Resting with Angels

As I sit here, I ponder, coffee in hand,
My mind; it has wandered towards a far, distant land.
Up there, where your Soul lies in peaceful slumber.
Resting with angels, surrounded by God's ethereal wonder.

Fervently we gather now, with prayerful laughter.
Eager; henceforth, to recall you, with affection,
Rich and vibrant with passion.
While embracing your thoughtfulness,
Through our birdsong joyfulness.

Hope is filling us up, dear Eamonn.
We feel you and your indefinable worth,
For you will never, ever be forgotten.
And you, expressing to us to weep no more!
But only smile with grace, upon your face!

You fill us up, like a sip, from your teacup!
Fully radiant, with sparkling starbursts a glisten.
We will remember your adventures, and your joys in life.
Gladdened now to acknowledge your happiness in your afterlife!
You are awed, while you sleep with God. +

Sis Sinead

Please forgive me, I did you wrong.
And I lost you.
But my heart was broken all along.

Nothing now, but hoping with a prayer,
That you will echo back.
The love you once granted me is somewhere.
Help me soar once again with some loving feedback.

This you have done and repleted my soul,
But sorrow is mine, for the tears I cannot control,
At the news of your sufferings,
Where you fight to utter soft mutterings.

God, grant you continued strength and courage to win a new day.
So, I can fly to your side and shroud you with togetherness, I pray.
Alas, time did not allow the nearness of you,
Your dried lungs did not function, and you died too soon too.

Heart's Desire

Is it possible to find one's heart's love desire? Are they out there?
They too searching, with a heart that beats for the one who is rare?
Wishing and yearning with a soul-felt connection, consumed
with love's passionate fire?

Suddenly, like a dream ushering forth, they appear from out of
the mist,
Exuding that same passion, you cannot resist.
Without warning your life changes within the blink of an eye.
Brimming with heavenly "love droplets" from the spiritual sky.

Touched in an instant by this sacred gift, no longer adrift.
Forever changed with a knowing, deep, and swift.
This is real, this is the love of your life, husband, or wife.
They, your partner, your soulmate, shining with wondrous light.
As the North Star did on that sacred night.

When I look at you. . .

When I look at you, I smile, and reminisce for just a while.
You had flown across the sea, to finally meet me.

When I hold your hand, I feel, all our love inside is real.
We have travelled far and wide, and we stand side by side.

When I watch you watching me, I feel this electricity.
I will always believe in you, our relationship so true.

This joy we'll share forever.
Two hearts joined together.
Nothing's stronger than our love. We fit like a glove.

When I look into your eyes, I see our life and realize,
All the warmth you brought to me shines forth for all to see.

Now I close my eyes and dream,
And see your face, which shines serene.
Our children are our gift from above, the joy of all our love.

When I look at you, I smile, and reminisce for just a while.
You had flown across the sea, to finally meet me.
To finally meet me.

What to Do?

I am in a quandary now and wonder what to do!
I am between a rock and a hard place.
I am lonely, sad, and blue,
Wondering, do I say Adieu?
I wish for a better, happier life to happen,
But the sameness is churning about.
Spewing out the non-passion,
Like, from a teapot's spout.
I want to turn it all around,
But I have not the courage to walk that road.
Where would I go? Alas, I am worn down.
From carrying such a weight and load.
There are questions I ask in my mind,
But no answers come, and the silence is deafening.
I am alone and it feels unsettling.
For you, my husband, are blind.
This is disheartening and disconcerting!
For what I am yearning, is far reaching!
And the road grows more disturbing!
And I am almost on my knees beseeching!
Responsibilities weigh heavy on my shoulders,
And I am stuck here in the whirring present,
Trying desperately to make it feel less discontent.
When I look into the mirror, it tells me "To let go".

But I keep questioning, and I am filled with woe.
  My heart is breaking, and weakening,
  To all the dreams that have passed,
  That were filled with hope, trust, love, but now I feel aghast.
  And when I place my heart in my hands,
  To truly look deep within, silence is weeping.
  I hear the rhythm of past distant lands.
      Wailing like a Banshee!
  Am I to follow their Cries' Commands?

Broken

Youth, how fickle you are! Now gone; no more a twinkling star.
I cannot go back and live the life I could have chosen.
Hence, I sit here, every day, frozen.
I keep looking back, and doing so is awkward, because you are
      always there.
The love, the pain, the hurt, and the sorrow I cannot bear.
From this day forward, I am left alone, facing my affair.
We were *one* a long time ago.
A duet surreal, that I did let go.
What am I to do, my lover?
For I can no longer recover.
I gaze ahead and wonder what we could have had, and I turn away
Broken-hearted, realizing that what is now, is what I live today.
However, you keep coming back; and I am left hoping, ready to please.
You filled me up, like a sip from the glass of the wine we both
      drank with ease.
And the looks we shared were such a tease.
Our hearts are, now, no longer joined,
Unhappily, I remember the melody we once coined.
The only hope was in the past,
The choice I took has held me fast, to a life I now feel is wound
      in the past.
Heed me when I say, I love you like no other, for you are my lover.
Hear the whisper in my heart, that beats softly for you,
And I honestly know that this whisper is murmuring only for you.
We two will now be a memory, a bygone chance.
You and I once danced romance.
One! Two! Three! One! Two! Three!
One! Two! Three! One! Two! Three!

The Pain

The pain is overbearing!
And I wish for solace and caring.

The pain is no longer silent.
It has shaken my being so violent.

Please catch me if I fall,
For I cannot carry me at all.

Darkness overcomes me.
And its tendrils grasp around me.

I cry out and try to crawl.
But no one came, so I fell, once and for all.

My mind has lost its grip,
But I try to scratch out with my fingertip,
The words that broke with a bawl.
"I no longer want to live for the long-haul".

Splintering of Self

It came upon me like a burning fire, that set me crashing and
    spiraling down into Hell.
I shook, burned and split and could not quell my certain death knell.
Into a million earth-shattering pieces, I bubbled and burst,
For doomed was I; pulled by the Infidel to burn accursed.
Detestable and foul was the smell of the smoldering fire,
That engulfed me and roasted me with His red-hot molten fire.
He had taken all He desired, and devilry took my soul,
Leaving me dead; destroyed; a pitiful darkened bit of charcoal.
I am no longer human, but a ghostlike shell,
Doomed walking on earth, as a hideous black cell.
I tried in vain to seek my soul and replenish it with water.
But found I could not, anywhere; for I was no longer God's daughter.
Only drifting now in nightmare; amid Satan's bared despair!
Withered, and twisted like dearth, I no longer fed from earth,
But spewed out my death fear.
With bleak emotion, within His dark, dismal blear.

Rage

I count.
Hoping for the best, to gain much needed rest,
For time does heal, but I wish to feel real.

Alas, *rage* swirls in and mighty forces begin
To overtake and keep me feeling in a tailspin.

The *past* has now returned, and I must face it.
A fearful young child with many traumas I spit.
Have I the courage to pursue the truth?
And put to rest the pains of my youth?

Can I make that difference? To this I feel diffidence.
For my *rage* is raw, although the sores ooze deliverance.

And with truth, I am no longer ambivalent to the scars; or no
longer malcontent.
I breathe in life with freedom to augment.
The real world, I so desire:
Filled with acceptance, reassurance, and wisdom to inspire.

Lost

Have you ever found yourself adrift?
Not knowing when it is time to swing shift.
All I can say is, this is important and not to ignore,
For it is significant; the answer lies in my own heart's core.

There will be times when nothing makes sense,
When all I feel is intense.
The world is a jumble and getting through the chaos,
Feels like a matrix askew, filled with suffering's pathos.

My mind itself, sometimes cannot tell what is real,
And that is why another does assist to help reveal,
What is reality, so I do understand.
My heart opening, by their gentle guiding hand.

Many clues give some assistance,
To the existence
Of the sincerity exuding from my own heart's core,
Eager now to disclose, its offerings galore.

The touching moment brings to bare,
Momentous experience to share.
Flowing forth, so I can rediscover
What is true and henceforth recover.

No longer adrift, but hearing and sensing all that is uttered,
Compassion comes rushing in warmly, like one being mothered.
Filling me with abundance:
I no longer feeling disturbance.
Calm and ready to steer myself back to living; no longer mired
     in fear,
And rekindle all that I have lost.

The Future

So elusive, so hard to grasp.
I try, but cannot touch the tiny thread
That dangles there to clasp.
I long to reach towards it,
So, I can see my future lit.
But, with every step I take, I feel reticence.
It hangs there, slippery, beseeching,
Beckoning for me to try to keep reaching,
But still, I cannot touch it,
Only to see it hang there, in the far-off distance.
Gently, wisely in time, I commit,
Gaining some semblance of courage to feel faintly sure,
And attentive to the future, that still seems such a blur.
Oh, how it echoes to me, and aids me nourishment.
Gently my spirit rises and out pops persuasive encouragement.
Humbly, I dust off my qualms and fears.
Ready am I to welcome some trust in my future years.
Pouring self-love to heal and keep me well,
Within my heart, it surely doth dwell.
Trust enables me to reach this tiny thread,
This filament that embodies all of what lies ahead.

Kindness

Comfort me and be my friend.
Show me warmth to aid me mend.
Give me your heart!
So, I do not fall apart.

Make me smile!
To feel no exile.
Caress me with your soft touch
Of kindheartedness to make me such.

Entrust to me your tender care,
And wrap me safe, so I can bear
The blows and stings of life,
To gain contentment and thrive.

Kindness is sweet and kindness begets
More kindness, which the world sometimes forgets.

Mental Health

The Devil had caught me and did a number,
But I awoke at last from my slumber.
Having bipolar disorder and not being aware,
Of the pitfalls of my own nightmare,
Caused me to act outside my character.
Nothing did abate my pain, within my brain,
Until it was found that the sacred pills
Of Lamictal and Lithium steadied my ills.
Mental health sometimes feels like a teeter - totter.
But by abiding by the doctor's orders, your mind is refreshed
        with tingling splashing water.
You guzzle down the needed remedy,
To live healthy and hopefully with indemnity.

I am testament to what I have achieved.
My reverence for my life is to be believed.

Coming Home

I called; you answered.
Finally, I had found the courage to tell you I was shattered.
Shattered from the mistakes I had made,
And shattered from the life I had strayed.
You whispered how much you cared and wanted me back,
I whispered "I love you" in a soft gentle voice of shamed lilac.
"Come home, love, please come home," was your sweet answer,
     layered like a honeycomb.
I cried with humiliation and humbleness that you still wanted me
     home.
Oh, the joy of knowing your wish was my wish reassured.
No longer bereft of the sorrows and pains we had endured.

I soared through the clouds and hugged my heart.
Oh, the bliss of finally watching for American soil.
It was a soul's yearning, long, long months spent in turmoil.
Now I was flying towards my family, I had torn apart.
And as we landed, I crossed myself and said a prayer,
Trusting that love would conquer with a celebratory fanfare.
I strode fast from the gate, full of strength and giddiness.
And I was met by my young men and you, especially you,
As you wrapped me with warm kisses and my sons hugged me too.
I had arrived where I wanted to be, sturdy, smiling, alive, standing
     in abundant happiness.

Forgiveness

I watched the tears fall and felt your pain slowly rush.
Tear upon tear, your face revealed the heartaches within.
How could I continue to gaze and not touch your soft wet skin?
No darling: do not weep so, for my heart will surely crush.

Was I the judge? Yes, but later No!
Our Hearts did break and were left fallow.
Our Roots shook deep from out our soil.
Our Seeds no longer planted, but left spoil.

Light dimmed, and darkness spread.
A furrow delved deep within our souls.
We both adrift; then filled with woes,
Of sorrow and bewilderment, alas, we no longer wed.

Life was meaningless and utter despair was rife.
No purpose left, only a broken life.
We called upon our wretchedness for thine own to come.
But no sound or whisper strummed.

However, God had not forsaken us,
For He carried us and placed His hand thus
Upon our hearts and we became found again,
Living within our own true love's domain.

Forgiveness comes in many guises,
But the one true forgiveness is granted,
When asked and comes when repentantly candid.
Unexpectedly, forgiveness wraps you snug, and empathy rises.

Yet I Am Worthy

My journey has brought me to a place of self-reflection.
One where I have delved deep and found a connection,
As to why so much has happened to me, and why not me?
It was to understand that I am human, and life has no guarantee,
Of turning out as I wanted it to be.
But still, I am worthy.

Nothing in life is truly white or black.
All I can do is to keep going and try.
And it is by doing I give back,
Even though through hard times I did cry.
Still, I am worthy.

I recall all my quirks and hurts.
And the hurt I did to others and my family.
For these I take full responsibility.
Yet, I am worthy.

Getting up is what is needed,
Even when I feel defeated.
Yes! I am worthy.

Walk talk and smile because you are so worthwhile.

Relationship

I do not know what to say or do,
Needing to impress, but all I feel is stress.
My mind is overwhelmed with thoughts and feelings,
That beat within my pounding heart.
How will it be possible to plead my part?

Being honest and true is the only way.
To impart my heart's true feelings this day,
By saying what lies therein,
And our love to begin again.

Nervously my hands fumble and start to sweat.
Deodorant and mouthwash are my duet.
Buzzing with excitement, I feel so alive and nervous,
And pray that this time will taste of honey, and we will flourish!

Life's Dream

I held it in my hands and let it go,
To waft through the air, Intermingling with the universe.
Hoping with a prayer,
That it would serve its purpose.
And provide some experience of tasty cream,
To the one who sought it out,
And found it was their own life's dream.
A dream rich in essence of life's teachings.
A dream filled with swirls of giddiness,
That convey to the mind, certain feelings,
Of joy, trust, and happiness' dizziness.
Everyone has a dream, some still a sunbeam.
But my dream is you and through you,
We found that we are *one* again, and our love as profound,
As the first day we met. With some regret.

I Have Found the One
My Soul Doth Love

I have found the one my soul doth love.
And I rejoice, for it is wonderful beyond measure.
My soul coos peacefully, like a dove.
And I feel gratitude, bursting with pleasure.

My heart is alive with overflowing fervor.
For the one that fills my being with love.
No other can surpass my own life's preserver,
For you are my champion, my darling dove.

God has granted my wishes galore!
And I thank Him, with all my heart.
My love is like a red, red rose and more.
Tenderly afire, and we, no longer apart.

Hear me when I say, you are the love of my life.
You are who God ordained.
For you are revered, and I am so happy to be your wife.
And we, my king, my scepter, are both deliciously changed.

How Do I Love Thee?

I love thee as brilliant as a new dawn rising from the earth,
Spreading its colors to form shadows and mists, yielding a
    rebirth.
A spectacle so beautiful, it moves one to tears.
My love for you is like a bloom that grows all through the years,
And smelling their perfume is truly awesome,
Intoxicating forever, and comfy like the sun.

The beauty of your eyes, sparkle and glimmer, and twinkle with joy.
They bestow qualities of trust and goodness; their powers do employ.
Mine own eyes see the flourish of a wondrous peace,
A gathering togetherness, that never ceases, through union's release.
Your love touches the tranquility of my soul,
And my love gushes forth and doth extol.

Like the oceans, wide and deep, is my love that breathes in and out,
Flowing and building, thus cascading in the tide's roundabout.
Even through the tempests, it cannot deny the loving in my heart
    I doth bestow.
Stable and steady it stands with the momentous winds and
    waves that blow,
Back and forth my love for you swirls with a musical tempo.
My heart sings the sweet melody with quality and purely sung tone,
Inspiring commitment to soothe your heart, which is a magical
    gemstone.

Intoxication!

Honeysuckle bursts!
Entice thirst!

And lavender balms!
Oh, doth calms!

Sweet rose meanderings!
Suggest love's philandering's!

And crocus, with bluebells delicacy!
Kiss my tender cheek elegantly!

Thy perfumes lingerings envelope me.
And swept, am I, into a dream of thee.

I see thy grace and beauty swoon.
Regal and mysterious as is the moon.
You waft through the air and shower your sprinkles spree,
Until thy intoxication of me.

My Love

You came to me as in a dream.
I saw you and I fell.
You were and still are the love of my life.
The one my heart doth dwell.

The years have passed, and we are here,
Still loving, still wanting, still feeling.
We, no longer alone, but still cleaving.
Oh, how I love you my dear.

When I look into your eyes,
I see the love you have for me.
It has not changed.
I will always be with you through the rough and the smooth.
My love, it is not feigned.

Come close, please closer still!
What do you hear?
It is my heart beating always for you,
And God above knows you are my heart, dear.

Family

Gathering round the table we all begin to talk, laugh, and smile.
It is something we all have not done in such a while.
Not a moment goes by where each reminisce of bygone times or
    chat about the day,
And we all listen with intent to what each other does say.

Looking upon the scene, love can be felt in all its glory.
For our faces reveal their inner passions that tell their own story.
No one is perfect and we acknowledge our difference in humor
    and good cheer.
We feel happy and content when we are gathered near,
And find these connections so dear.

Sisters, brothers, aunts and uncles, nieces, nephews, husbands,
    and wives all clamor to be heard.
We revel in the warmth and excitement of our lives that had occurred.
And we cry through the tragedies and pain we all shared,
To try to find the meaning in life in what we all were unprepared.

However, through the good and bad, pain and joy,
We have gathered once again to be at home and just enjoy.
What matters most is we still feel connected, and we never doubt,
Who we are and what we are all about!
For family is love and love is a family forever.

It Is Well with My Soul

As you have read and understood, I have faced many difficulties.
But with strength, my troubles wound many efficacies.
Staying steadfast to what I knew was possible.
The outcome became truly phenomenal.

I learned that fear was part of courage.
The kind that springs the mind to flourish.
Not stopping dead in our tracks,
But having the will to do it anyway, and face all the facts.

Somehow, somewhere I gained a new appreciation,
Of all that lay inside of me.
True grit was my fortified key.
I had found the willingness to prosper with honest celebration.
And I am well now, and I avow,
It is well.
It is well with my soul.

Health Is Wealth

The best kind of wealth is health.
No other conscious thing in life is so important,
For to be concordant to your purpose and not to lie dormant.
One's mind, body, and soul can reflect a peace,
That can bless one's gentle heart to sing with release.
When you are well you can do almost anything.
You rise and welcome whatever the day doth bring.

What is health, but your wealth.
This is the key to one's happiness and success.
An allegiance to this I profess.
A key to keeping safe, warm, and aglow.
While with time you learn to not let go. Hold on and be smart.
To live in healthy wealth within your heart.

Abiding Love

Abiding love, resolute, unwavering.
Holds me up, keeps me strong, even when I am failing.
Steadfast and firm is Your faithfulness and love.
Thank you, God, for all You do and give from up above.

Abiding love, warm and tender-hearted.
Always there, never fails, when I'm broken-hearted.
I pray to You; feel your sustenance and care.
Thank you, God, for all You do, it helps when I can share.

Abiding love, confident and always true.
Endless trust; constant love; keeps me close to You.
Ceaseless and poised is Your hand that holds onto mine.
Thank you, God, for all You do because you are divine.

Imagine

Imagine for a moment you felt afraid and insecure.
Imagine an angel coming down from heaven to reassure.
Imagine all their beautiful light filling your soul.
Imagine you floating up high and being whole.
Imagine all that you could be.
Imagine this and feeling free.
It would be a miracle without a doubt,
God's intent to help you not feel without.

Imagine for a moment, you felt alone and exposed.
Imagine God's hand reaching down to help you feel composed.
Imagine all His love surrounding your body.
Imagine Him telling you, you are worthy.
Imagine this and feeling perfect.
Imagine His love with upmost respect.
It would be a miracle beyond all measure.
God's eternal love we can all treasure.

"Let there be light."

Light suffused the earth with prisms' sparkling delight.
Bursting forth with rays of hope, that flashed a wondrous light.
This light shone luminous with God's heavenly goodness,
To become our escort; thus, overshadowing all darkness.
Colors created beautiful, arose multifaceted from the depths within.
So, blessed the earth and every living thing.
White light was made our day,
To illuminate and suffuse our own life's journey's way.
An energy force, brimming with wisdom,
Illuminating down, from God's heavenly kingdom.
Powerful diffusions of beauty, pulsated a Holy vibration,
With wondrous profusions of God's bountiful creation.
Light blazing intensely, with His glorious approbation.
God's proclamation; His passionate jubilation.

God's Love

God's love cares not for garish platitudes,
That spring forth, devoid of warm, compassionate attitudes.
Arrogance, conceit, or skepticism,
Are not accepted, among despot cynicism.

We are all part of God's divinity,
Chosen to wash away selfish imagery,
With sanguine dignity and affinity.
For God's Love is nurturing, kind with simplicity.
Gifted to us freely; His Love's one divine, sustaining mystery.

Holy Trinity; Jesus, Spirit, God in One,
Lies within us; God's luminous Love, deep-seated in everyone.
Share this, this sacred unity.
Born of you, to transform hatred into love.
Reverberating with magnanimity and equanimity,
Atoned by Him from up above.
God's Love blesses the heart and touches the soul,
With humble acceptance and whole-hearted self-control.

Letting Go and Letting God

When one considers all God's remarkable wonders of life,
One comes to realize how magnificent they beckon like a tuneful
    fife.
Letting go is to be loved abundantly with nature's soft, caressing
    kisses.
Even in life's journey filled with lessons, weaved by God's eternal
    wishes.

God's word is refreshing.
God's love is a blessing.
God's breath is within us to breathe kindheartedly.
God's wisdom glows within us too,
Encouraging us, to live good-heartedly.

No guile has He.
Letting God is to be free.
Goodness and mercy spring forth from the earth.
Thus, letting God, the divine, light up our worth.

Prayer

Goodwill, instill.
Listen, and be still.
Sense the quietude,
That brings bearing to the solitude.

Now enters peace,
With a steady release,
Speak with emotion,
And devotion,
For your entreaties are heard.
Soothed by God's soft, caressing word.
Deep within, your pleas will be answered, because you do believe.
No prayer goes unanswered because to God you doth cleave.

God stirs you to awaken and have fortitude,
To keep on going and have a determined attitude.
Your Faith will shield you.
Your Trust will empower you.
Your Prayers will be fulfilled too.

For God wraps you warm,
Whilst transforming your prayers into full form.

Spring Is Here

O the joys of springtime, watching new life spring forth.
And the honeybee swarming about, pollinating all the flowers
    that sprout.
Feeling overjoyed by the beauty surrounding you, spreading its worth.
And breathing in the perfumes of new life all about.

Be busy in your garden growing,
And stand in the sheer majesty of it all showing,
Whilst finding a connection where rebirth begins.
Dancing and yielding to a spirit warm and tender, that wins.
A new cycle swirls, so you can create,
The new life you yearn and dream about and cannot abate.
Pluck stems here and there and everywhere,
And make bouquets of love for thine own self to share.

Hope

Ever wonder what holds you up?
It is Hope!
Ever wonder what encourages you on your way?
It is Hope!
Ever wonder what keeps you going?
It is Hope!
Ever wonder what supports you through each day?
It is Hope!

Inside you is something worth believing and achieving.
Inside you is something worth tending and defending.
Inside you is something worth caring about and sharing.
Inside you is something worth living and forgiving.

Never stop wishing, or yearning.
Never stop praying and discerning.
Never stop loving or daring.
Never stop asking and learning.

Look up and about, walk tall and have no doubt!
Trust, and be confident in what life's all about!

There *is hope*,
An assurance you cannot live without!

Faith

Believe in the unseen, with hope in your heart,
And it *will* come to pass, for faith *is* a huge part.
We are all created to carry a light,
Never to be alone; but feeling bolstered through our plight.

Faith is not something you can touch, or see,
But *is* there, yearning to be carried forth,
For it has value, merit and worth,
Built from your conviction to become a true reality.

You, too, have been given a seed to assist you along,
Helping you to grow, while mustering courage to walk through
    your trials.
Faith spreads its sustained essence, sprinkling comfort with smiles,
Enabling you to travel onward, knowing that you belong.

Faith leaves no one, for it has power profound,
Culminating with a god-like force,
To illuminate man's course,
Revealing wisdom its place where, faith doth abound.

Grace

Grace stands splendid, radiating outwards toward man.
Welcoming and warm; her rays swirling like a fan.
Grace needs no words, as she knows the soul so well.
For grace is holy, manifest from God, and in your heart doth dwell.

Grace embraces all your transgressions, and confessions,
Granting you forgiveness in God's divine plan.
Helping you to transform and be blessed, so you do all you can.

Grace helps you to believe in your possibilities more and more,
Not leaving you poor or wounded in your own heart's core.

Grace fills you with divine good spirits from above.
Grace forever open, creates her charms with love,
Knowingly guiding you gently into port,
So, fear is no longer your escort.

Grace is all-encompassing, fully aware.
Grace beckons all to taste her wondrous fare,
For grace does as God grants.
His mercy through His son was for all, and not perchance.

Compassion

Breathe!
Concede to the rhythmic lead
Of your heart filling with a passionate thirst,
For the deep compassion waiting to burst!

Feel the fervent release of love expanding,
Filling your soul with warm understanding.

Mankind can shine from empathy,
Without enmity, emitting within.

Allow the passion of compassion,
To fill the recesses of your soul.
Let it be your goal.
You can heal when you feel.

The heart of man can transform,
To be the most beautiful individual,
And this is pivotal.

As compassion is key to kindness,
For in it lies forgiveness and guidance.

Trust

Trust is belief, that does not lie in disbelief.
It enhances the senses and begets relief.
Trust is a promise, that assures your every word,
And builds, to establish your character, and accord.

Trust is comfort you wrap yourself cozy, with warm self-confidence,
Ensuring a glow that attracts a stream of good self-worthiness.
Trust is integrity you stand in, for one and another in life,
To withstand ignobleness and strife.

Trust is strength you gather when faced with adversity,
Or on the brink of uncertainty,
To aid you when crestfallen,
Gaining your stature, to rest your weary heads in.

Trust, you rely on, which does not shadow fear.
Bolstering courage when hard times are near.
Trust is a welcome you embrace without an ounce of rebellion.
Thus, summoning a feeling that all will be well,
While you wait for the sound of news, you are unable to quell.

Trust is an experience you feel, with shining zeal,
When you look into the eyes of a loved one or a friend,
That wends warmth, like a glowing fire, and they a godsend.

Trust is an emotion you feel, firm in the certainty,
That purposely portends prosperity.
Trust is like a fragrance, sweet of perfume, releasing from your being,
That scents through the air, on all humanness,
With a deep-seated rootedness.

Trust is confidence you gain through knowledge, to keep you resilient,
Strong with perseverance, that glimmers brilliant.
And join with human masterminds,
To create unity and affirm true alliance.

Respect

Do not fly from me or make me less.
Stay clothed in me and be mine own comforts compress.
For You do matter and point the way,
To consider not just me, but all others in a kind way.

Resist all pride and conceit.
Do not quibble or be filled with deceit.
Drink of reverence and sense, with a dignified manner,
To lend some peace, in thine own prized, esteemed banner.

All are significant and come into play, In life's choice runway.
For You gift goodwill toward man,
To enhance meaning and appreciation through one's own lifespan.

Honesty

Do not grapple with notions of unfounded anxieties and cares.
Seek truth among the web of entangled lies.
Continue in strength to walk in your power, with conquering airs.
For time is the great revealer and oh so wise.

Honesty cup shall overflow and cascade forth.
Streaming its water to cleanse and establish new growth.
True honesty is a wisdom optimistic and full
Of decency, integrity, and dignity, layered soft, like cotton wool.

Honesty is an asset that completes a virtuous attribute.
Honesty is a worthy act of straightforwardness that is fair.
Honesty and honor, ring a legacy of repute,
Against lies, and disarming deceptions, to serve one's moral welfare.

Wisdom

Wisdom grows from understanding and knowledge,
Born of fruit's experience, and warm accepting homage.

Wisdom is a willingness to think non-judgmentally,
Which brings kindness, growing exponentially.

Wisdom carries with it insight, and care.
That is virtuous and fair.

Wisdom enlightens and is a perception optimistic,
Hence insights prove to be altruistic.

Wisdom lies within you; you born to learn,
And the gifts of goodness to discern.

Wisdom brings benevolence, kindness, and forbearance,
That smarts at scorn, derision, and intolerance,
Thus, behooving of sufferance endurance.

Wisdom is golden!
A gift beholden!
In heart's sincerity!
Yielding prosperity!

Humility

Are you meek in the swirls of doing and receiving?
Do you understand yourself and are you discreet?
Do you give thanks to do your best without pride or conceit?
Do you accept your weaknesses and strengths with modest
    achieving?

Humility is the virtue of virtues.
It enables you to acknowledge that you must be humble,
In all with which you have been blessed and not grumble,
When trials ask you not to exploit or abuse.

It is a garnering virtue to bow in genteelness,
Because you choose this with measured eagerness.
Your composure gifted to be true tenderness,
And your knowledge to browbeat pretentiousness.

Humility is not boastful, or full of your own verbosity.
Humility is a modesty in self-control,
To live your life in dignified civility, with generosity.
And be discreet with a lush heart and soul.

Happiness

To be happy one must count on a moment.
One that you hold, like a keepsake, a precious bestowment.
Your heart loving: your mind honeyed as the sun.
Where happiness is pleasure with delights richly heart spun.

The days and nights whirl around; glad to be part of it all.
No longer lost, but free to feel the bursts of happiness cascade
    like a waterfall.
Living each day with gratitude and smiles, which stirs a wellness
    inside.
For rich are you in spirit, with sparkling eyes that gleam wide-eyed.

Happiness can be counted in love, laughter, and warm hugs.
Happiness comes from the heart, touched by nature's abounding
    floods,
Of colors, charms, scents, and beauty that you warmly embrace.
Thus, happiness is a bounteous well, that overflows with a heart-
    warming grace.

Joy

When you hold a newborn babe in your arms, your heart is filled
with Joy.
'Tis His miracle, by which His love's succor you doth enjoy.

When you look into the eyes of man, you see the immense
majesty of their soul.
The glory of God's magnificent affection doth extol.

To see a blazing sunset at night is Joy personified,
For its splendor holds you spellbound to feel Holy mystified.

Sitting on a mountain top and seeing the beauty all around.
One knows that Heaven most assuredly mirrors its vistas surround.

Appreciating art in all its forms, leaps your spirits into a magical
realm,
Of Joyful sensitivity and overpowering, emotional whelm.

Christmas brings a warm glow, that emanates throughout the world,
Creating a togetherness of humankind, soliciting goodwill, that is
Joyfully swirled.

Love itself does wave and surge, as the rivers and oceans ebb
and flow,
But at its peak, Joy rises to a plateau.

Joy means delight, wonder, gladness, and bliss.
So, it is blessed by a sweet, tender wish and kiss.

Feel the pleasure and enjoyment of every moment,
For you will travel through life with purpose and contentment.

Joy is golden, rich with treasure, beyond all measure.
It fills your heart and soul with appreciation, and a wondrous
    adventure.

Empathy

Come close and listen to my heart.
It is scalded with hurts that smart,
Which leaves me moaning with sorrows,
That have carved pains like arrows.
What am I to do, dear life?
Is there someone who will not writhe in the knife?
Surely there is someone!

Empathy is a deep emotional connection for another's sorrows
     and pain,
By being present and feeling tender-hearted, without disdain.

Empathy is sitting and listening without judgement or rebuke,
Thus, allowing respect and dignity to dwell, as a heartfelt attribute.

Empathy is giving your hand with comfort and understanding,
To bring about relief, while sustaining the living heart there standing.

Empathy is being that friend who truly feels compassion.
To care intensely and continue to support with devotion and
     enthusiasm.

Empathy is affection in its greatest form.
A heart pouring when hard times swarm.

Gratitude

Graceful attitude, I find in thee.
A source that is good inside of me.
A gratefulness that I bestow.
For all the gifts You sweetly flow.

My heart speaks of thankfulness for all You have done.
And I feel a recompense to do for others, one by one.
My appreciation for my life is, in essence, won,
Whence amends are hence pleasing, and divinely spun.

Gratitude I deeply feel.
Your blessings I know are real.
Your positivity is shone,
On each and every one.

O dear gratitude, I pay homage to thee,
For my soul and person are beholden to thee.

Patience

Anger does not lie in thee, sweet patience.
Only stillness that wafts bouquets of pure obedience.
No restlessness is felt when troubles come.
Simply an acceptance of what is the outcome.

Sit with endurance and a soul urged to pause.
For moderation is chief, in life's journey's cause.
Temper yourself and feel calm,
When irritation and annoyance seek to qualm.
Pursue serenity with harmony, for you will find.
Goodwill and even-tempered care, entwined.

Patience is a virtue that one struggles with daily,
To finally learn without complaint,
That life is full of choices that are met bravely,
So, you can live in comfort and not feel constraint.

Strength

Strength rises like the phoenix when you need it the most.
It carries you strong through hardships and tribulations,
And stands firm to withstand all sufferings, foremost.
In strength lies a stoicism that builds mighty foundations.

Strength asserts your mind, so you can reason with clarity.
Strength powerfully acknowledges your potential and charity.

It is a staunch strength that grants you courage,
To live with fortitude and flourish,
That proves to you, that you can succeed,
To live a life filled with determined intentions in both word and deed.

Self-Esteem

Look with daring and self-confidence,
Upon your image of loveliness and know that providence
Ensures no quiver of shame lie among the vast array of thoughts,
That succor your soul to feel alive, where life again feels like
    sparkling sunspots.

You feel full of self-assurance for who you are and what you
    learned about yourself.
You stand strong with a great sense of self-worth upon yourself.
No insecurities are felt because you deem yourself valuable and
    appreciated,
And you walk regal, wrapped in self-respect, and feel comfortably
    emancipated.

Courage

Do not shiver in fear, but lift thy heart with pluck upon that which
    doth scares you.
Gather your mind to face head-on the dreads that seem to
    overcome you.
Feel the pulse of grit spread through you.
And do not shed a tear or mourn the past parts of you.

Courage stands in its glory.
Not shy, but full of heart's willingness to charge forward,
Not to look back but move with determination upon the blue
    horizon onward.
And conquer that which is simply a step congratulatory.

Courage has a valiant heart:
A heart that is yours apart.
Take that leap of true daring, for you will be glad,
For your life is intended and you will no longer be sad.

Soul's Journey

What lies within *you*?
What is it *you* feel inside?
Are *you* motivated, hopeful and ready too?
Trust and get going; for your soul, is your guide.

Listen to your need!
For *you* are born to succeed.
You have something unique.
Wealth within,
And integrity tuned as a violin,
Waiting and brimming to burst with mystique.

When *you* were born, joy filled the world.
Heavenly energy pulsed with love.
Spirit and soul ignited with light!
Bursting a life force, stunningly pearled!
You are somebody!
You are worthy!
Significant! Powerful!
Potent and Alive!
Predestined to Thrive.

Have grit!
Commit! Do not quit!
You have what it takes!
Push through!
Have faith! Do not wait!
Pray now for all you desire— And be that fire!
For your destiny awaits—

Soul's Light

Your soul is an intrinsic beauty of your body.
It sheds a profound light within, for you to embody.
Your Soul's light is unique to everyone else.
And doesn't shine any the less.
Not similar, but a burst of energy, like a hot compress.
It gifts bright when you love, give, and inhale.
Spiritual breath to encourage you to grow and prevail.
Your soul's light is the love you have for yourself,
And the light needs to glow brightly around you.
Your light is full of glory, emanating from within oneself,
To show how wonderful you are too.
It was bestowed on you to share with the world to imbue.
The soul calls to you to follow your life purpose in your lifetime,
Motivating you forward to accomplish and give over time.
A soul designed with divine essence and as bright as the sun.
A reverence for life, where soul's light is the outcome.

Soul's Peace

Come, sit awhile, and listen to your gentle voice murmurings.
Melodious silence is sweetly heard.
The peaceful whisperings of soft, quiet solitude enter with
    genteel nurturing's.

Feel the rhythms of ripening peace flowing deep within,
Awakening the soul to repose, and nurture therein.
Allow peace to softly vibrate its tuneful echoes,
Through your own mind's heart's mementos.

Calm serenity permits "Times" true reflections.
To sooth your reticence and arouse your affections.
Allow peace to embrace and envelope you with steadfast readiness,
And encompass you wholly, with warm genteelness.
Hence all anxiety and mind's stress are quelled. So, you embrace
    peace that quietened and swelled.
Repose is some blessed peace,
Welcomed by life's energy's sweet release.

Feelings

To feel is rich, as emotions convey that you are alive.
They ride the crests of waves that are in constant motion,
Filling you with questions, that brings a solution.
They stir, within the depths of your sacred shrine, to nurture and
      thrive.

Feelings are always present inside you.
They encourage you to stand robust too,
While you gain insights, through reflection, amid your wanderlust,
Ensuring your search to reach acceptance, serenity, peace, and trust.

Tears, laughter, anger, love, happiness, sorrows, kindness or remorse,
Are but a few provoking emotions that swirl around, depending
      on your course.
Feelings support you to master a reverence for life,
Even when you struggle through painful strife.
Henceforth spiritually aware; you grow into your full heart.
Finally, becoming God's entirely realized "Holy Work of Art."

War

Thump! Boom! Rattle! Fear!
Is the coast clear?
Crawling, digging, running, killing.
Is my time near?
Heads down, shrapnel flying.
Breathing, moaning, screaming, dying.
Cold, chaos, crying, mourning.
Never ending raindrops pouring.
Mud, sludge, grime, slide, nowhere for one to hide.
Hunger, aching, panic, pain.
Darkness, shadows, night, slain.
Scared, terror, horror, dread,
Not one place to set one's head.
Chance, peril, fate!
Alas too late! Hatred, fight,
God help us in our plight.

Our World Today

We wish we could be at peace.
We wish for better days.
We wish the world showered rays of kindness,
By which happiness it conveys.

Nothing seems to make sense anymore.
Nothing yields a solution.
All we wish is to be treated fair, with a genuine rapport,
Filled with dignity and tolerance, leading to universal resolution.

Let us show our respect and devotion,
For a new and meaningful way,
So, all can keep on living in harmonious motion.
Becoming the world, in which we can enjoy freely, day by day.

World! wake up!
Leap into trust and be fearless today!
Come on world!
Break the chains and do not delay.
Knowledge is our motivation, with no walls of famishment.
A world where we each feel worthy,
To live among one another without controversy,
And to stand an impassioned inhabitant.

Awaken World!

Awaken, World!
Let love smite out unfairness.
Awaken World! And show You care.
Sense a clear and meaningful awareness,
That will enhance our own world's welfare.

War brings naught but heavy grief,
Killing hearts steeped bloody red,
Spewing out with hot molten hatred,
Fighting for a cause self-righteous, with no relief.
Leaving only undeniable, painful conflict and blight,
Empty of compassionate and enlightening foresight.

What we must do is listen with willingness and encouragement,
Built on understanding and unflustered attainment.
Giving thought to every side and establishing coherence.
A gifting adherence with humane forbearance.
Stop! Take heed! Look to your own affairs,
And rediscover our world's living luminaires.

Sisters

Sisters are the sustenance of life.
The ones you can count on to listen through your strife.
Sisters gather round the table,
And exude a love that keeps you stable.

Sisters calm the waves of anxiety,
And carry the salve that mends, without piety.
They embrace your weakness,
And empower your uniqueness.

Sisters love you when you are mad or glad.
They help you laugh through the good and the bad.
They are the pillows you lay your head on,
When all friends are gone.

There is no other friend who is closer.
A sister is a bond, a living bolster,
You can hold with love and smile,
And feel you are worthwhile.

Paula

You are the one who is strong of mind.
Always doing and giving in kind.
Keeping everyone and everything afloat,
Strong character and a smile to note.
You are soft of heart and firm of will.
And find time to travel and explore still.

You are the light of your children's eye.
And the love of one other, who is so dear.
You are my sister, who is truly sincere.
In all you do and say, by the by.
Your heart is, as you are, as warm as the sun.
And your spirit is wholeheartedly spun.

Catherine

The day you were born was heaven personified.
A day of sunshine and joy amplified.
You are gorgeous as a rose,
And our hearts are warmly close.
You give with compassionate care.
Your heart tender, from which you do share.

Your words touch everyone,
In a way that speaks benevolence won.
You are strong in a way that spins like a song.
Echoing strings of harmony, from which we know we belong.
You are the one on whom all else rely,
For you give comfort and love with an endless supply.

Friend

You walked into my life, quietly sat, and just talked.
It was a charming time and quite unexpected.
We enjoyed the repartee, as we connected,
Grateful for the moments we reflected.

You, a good listener, a friend that was special.
This gift not in everyone, but so essential
To make one feel that life has potential,
No matter the circumstance; or how stressful.

As you sat and listened and looked at me,
I felt a semblance of serenity wash over me.
Your sensitivity sharpened and I must agree,
That in those moments, a calm came over me.

I do not know why this happened!
I have no answers; but my heart felt gladdened.
Still life is strange and somewhat preordained.
And as we said goodbye, I felt sustained.

Pastor Lynn

The day had come!
My prayers to God made fast.
"Let this be where I'm meant to stay,
And reveal to me Your cast."

I did not know what would happen.
Nor if you would approve.
But the hope within my heart you would see,
The answer lay with me.

With each question that was asked.
I felt Him play a chord.
For as I uttered every word,
He smiled peacefully His accord.

He had come and sat among us that day.
And quietly wielded His intent.
His guiding hand He tendered us,
And bestowed what was meant.

You questioned and observed me.
I never thinking with record.
You would come to represent so much,
And friendship is our reward.

We two are very much entwined.
And you are the one who will always be,
A true expression of womankind,
For your benevolence extended to me.

Louise Catherine

You sat beside me on the first day of a new school year.
You were kind and watched me and gently asked me my name.
We played outside and our friendship grew steadfastly sincere.
And as we blossomed, our bond became strong like a soulmate
flame.

You are the connection to the past, the present, and the future.
And when you speak, you speak with authority and gladdened
good humor.
You are the light that still glows, which strengthens everyone
you touch.
The lioness protector, when hard times come knocking, when I
feel nonplussed.
You are the wisdom tree that carries burdens through tunnels in
my life.
You are the sprinkling stardust that grants me hope, for me to cope.
You jolt me forwards with warm tastings of a good scintillating wine,
Reminding me, of the good times gone and the memories still
to shine.
You are my truest friend and when we talk, we just start where
we left off.

Molly

You are a ray of sunshine, who walks and talks with a strong
    devotion to all you wish to heal.
Your sword of truth cuts through the chafe and confusions,
And like a mother, you gently caress the wounds of many who
    have delusions.
Your instinct prevails and with a commanding, tender passion,
    you reveal what is real.

Your heart sways to and fro, with a nimbleness that's kind.
And your voice breathes a deep regard for all who come your way.
You joke with a decency of heart, so all can be relieved of pains
    of the mind.
And to find their way, they laugh with you, as your conclusions
    do allay.

I sit and admire your wondrous gifts, to touch one at their own
    heart's core.
To be my friend is my blessing from above.
That you should walk into my life and make it so much more.
Our time is a treasure, and your beauty of soul and eyes are a
    fullness thereof.

Thought . . .

I felt something stir in me.
A gentle flicker of inquiry.
I was called into consideration to name,
Where this dreamy notion came.

This flicker weaved born an idea.
Its thread still not understood,
Though its conception flowed through my mind.
Holding my attention, spinning like silvery silk wood.

Sensed as a spark, imagination impressed my brain.
Growing with determination and consideration.
Like a spider weaving its silky cobweb.
Gently, yet swirling, a brilliant "Young Deb".
Fascination danced, and out sprung inspiration,
Like a bubbling champagne,
Effervescent; a delightful cognition.

Rain

Rain, rain, come today.
Come, so I can swirl and play.
Let me dance in your showers,
And feel your cleansing powers.

Come, lovely rain.
Sprinkle my heart wet.
Drench me with your drips, drops duet.
And touch my soul and make it thrive,
Free from the vicissitudes of life.

Let me plop, splatter and splash, with no care in the world.
Let me burst with joy and hug these moments of time.
Let me lie in your puddles with raindrops splurged,
To laugh with delight and glee, like you are in a child's pantomime.

Come, rain, shower on me, and love me free.

Twilight

Daylight fades and turns to you, luscious twilight.
You strike the coming of night with a warm sultry glow.
It is then we delight and behold your dazzling show.
We marvel how you cast your shadows and twinkling gifts below.

You amaze the eye with your colors sublime,
While you swirl a vista in your twilight's serene time.

You embrace the light, then gently fade into night.
But before you close, you wave us quiet!
Sun rests within your soft hue,
To gently wave the day adieu.

Beauty Moon

At night I sit and watch your glows,
That prepares the way to another day.
You move and send shafts of lighted shadows.
Among our earthen highways.
You set the times of tides and hours of light for us to feel and see.
And most times you glow stately, in your own majesty.

Intuition feasts and darkened secrets emerge into play.
Reflections channel through the chafe and become a dazzling
    display,
Where despair and darkness ceases to crinkle the wounds of the
    heart.
Your shining insight and enlightenment spool a renewed,
    refreshing start.

O moon, you come and dance to your silvery lights.
Wrapped in your celestial beauty's devised mystical nights.

Daylight Bright

Daylight breaks; and the sun
Spreads its golden rays over everyone.
O how wonderful it is to awaken and feel you spread your
      wondrous beaming light too.
Upon my face, as I stretch wide today,
To say, "Good morning, sweet day."

You are the light that is full of sunbeams,
Full to the brim of daily dreams.
You conquer dark and display a mastery full of possibilities,
Where everyone can leap into doing and revel in their own
      capabilities.
Thus saying, "Thank you for your beauty spray."

O Daylight bright, I welcome thee.
You are my companion's gift in sustaining me.

Here Comes the Sun

Here it comes!
See it peek through the clouds of strife.
It is the sun, in all its glory, brimming with life.

Allow the warmth of the sun to bathe you cozy,
And your cheeks to feel rosy.

May the beams of light dance upon your face with delight!
And bring your harvest, to whet your appetite.

Laugh, smile, dance and have fun.
Shine your rays bright, like the Sun!
And be Kind to everyone!

Blessings

Blessings upon you.
Blessings upon your family and upon your friends too.
Blessings on your life.
Blessings be the warmth of your spirit that will thrive.
Blessings to those who weep.
For all heartaches are felt deep.
Blessings to those who suffer.
For they shall be comforted as a lover.
Blessings be upon all who need.
For all shall be sustained in deed.
Blessings to those who are afraid.
May love and peace be displayed.

'Tis Blessings I hold dear in my heart.
Even when I do depart.
For You do wondrous things
And grant Your blessings on all our wings.

Yvonne studied voice at Dublin's College of Music, Dublin, Ireland, and later continued studies in London, on a grant from Guinness Mahon Bank. For six seasons, she was leading soprano for Jury's Irish Cabaret, Ireland and took part in three major coast-to-coast tours of the USA and Canada with Columbia Artists. She also sang at Westbury Fair. She appeared at Dublin's Gaiety and Olympia Theaters, had many appearances with the Irish radio orchestra and concert orchestra, broadcast *Riders to The Sea* for BBC and PBS, and performed with Irish Operatic Repertory Company of Cork, with Scottish Opera, Dublin Grand Opera and at the Wexford Opera Festival. She met her husband, Richard Crist, at the Wexford Opera, and later moved to New York City. Shortly after the birth of their son Patrick, she was to fulfill a childhood dream, playing Eliza in *My Fair Lady* in Europe. Not only did she have the opportunity to co-star with British TV star, Tony Anholt and international film and theater star Maximilian Schell, but did so in Munich, Vienna, Berlin, Hamburg, Frankfurt, Amsterdam, Rotterdam, Den Haag and Antwerp, to unanimous praise from the European press. Yvonne now has a second son Daniel and lives in Athens, Ohio with her family. Writing has always been a passion and continues to bring her satisfaction every day.

Life can fall to the depths of despair.
And crumble into a million pieces.
But there is nothing you cannot bear,
With a little prayer,
As Time and Rhythm never ceases.
Life is a blessing, not a curse!
Be a part of this world for better or worse!
Life's not fair, but see, life is everywhere.

Why don't you stop; have a breather and take a moment to read through a few poems to relax you, uplift your spirits and discover the journey I took through the last Eight years of my life. This journey I was on was difficult and downright humbling, which granted me opportunities to pause, reflect, and write my thoughts and feelings down on the pages before you. Inside I know you will find something of interest that will awaken your soul, and maybe perhaps you will also find some solace through the difficulties you may have faced or are facing. Certainly, life can rock the bottom out of your world but know that life teaches us lessons. We need to take time out, recharge and be true to ourselves. You will find poems that will give you pause to ponder on all the abundance that we can embrace and believe that there is something truly spiritual at play. Poems that can inspire and embolden you to walk through your life with peace, courage, strength, and believe that you are a worthy human being.